WHEN
LIFE TURNS
UPSIDE
DOWN

WHEN
LIFE TURNS
UPSIDE
DOWN

Finding Stability through
God's Comforting Peace

John A. Younts

When Life Turns Upside Down:
Finding Stability through God's Comforting Peace

ISBN Paper: 978-1-63342-207-0
ISBN Epub: 978-1-63342-208-7
ISBN Mobi: 978-1-63342-209-4

To buy copies of this book in bulk at a special discounted price, inquire from the publishers below.

Shepherd Press | P O Box 24 | Wapwallopen | PA 18660
www.shepherdpress.com

Book cover design and typeset: www.greatwriting.org

Table of Contents

Over the years, Jay Younts has been my personal Gandalf, my Mr. Miagi, my Paul.
With fatherly wisdom and genuine care, Jay offers us this prayerful life-guide, showing us how to live life from God's perspective and not our own, keeping us right-side up in a world that feels upside down.

KIRK CAMERON
ACTOR, FILM PRODUCER

Younts turns our attention to hope found in the mercy of God and the provision he has made for mankind in the sinless life and sacrificial death of his Son, Jesus Christ. This book will provide encouragement and hope in these scary times.

DR. TEDD TRIPP
AUTHOR, PASTOR, CONFERENCE SPEAKER

Foreword

An Upside-Down World

The week of March 16, 2020, our world was turned upside down. By the end of the week, schools and businesses in the United States were forced to close. People were encouraged to avoid social gatherings. Scores of churches suspended corporate worship, choosing to provide virtual worship their congregants could access from home. Psalm 46 came to mind:

God is our refuge and strength,
    a very present help in trouble.
Therefore we will not fear though the earth gives way,

though the mountains be moved into the
heart of the sea,
though its waters roar and foam,
though the mountains tremble at its swelling.
Psalm 46:1–3, ESV

We are not the first generation to face a deadly pandemic. In the second century, smallpox claimed five million lives. Twenty-five million succumbed to the bubonic plague in the middle of the first century. In the middle ages, the same plague claimed another 75-200 million souls. Twice in the nineteenth century and once in the early twentieth century, cholera slew millions more. In 1918, Spanish flu accounted for up to fifty million deaths. We live in a dangerous world. Disease, suffering, and death are part of the curse under which fallen humanity lives out its days.

Of course, it is not only unknown pathogens that can turn our world upside down. As Job reminds us, *"Man is born to trouble as the sparks fly upward..."* Financial reversals, betrayal by friends, natural disasters, wasting illness, loss of loved ones, and all manner of circumstances can make us feel like the ground has fallen out from beneath us.

The realization that our lives can be turned upside down in a moment leaves us humbled and perplexed: humbled by our weakness and seeming insignificance, and perplexed about how to interpret and respond to circumstances that upend our lives. Jay Younts has done us a great service by bringing perspective rooted in God's unchanging truth. He reminds us that God is at work in all things for our good and for his glory. Younts turns our attention to hope found in the mercy of God and the provision he has made for mankind in the sinless life and sacrificial death of his Son, Jesus Christ. This book will provide encouragement and hope in these scary times.

Dr. Tedd Tripp
Author, Pastor, Conference Speaker

Introduction

Prayer Keeps Life Right-Side Up

This book is about living life from God's perspective and not your own. This cannot happen without consistent, informed, faithful prayer. Praying constantly for God's wisdom and discernment is a lifestyle habit that will keep your world balanced. Your heart can remain right-side up, regardless of the circumstances you encounter.

Paul commands all of us to pray constantly, continuously. To do this, we must see how God has prepared us in his Word, by his Spirit, to respond to the unexpected events of life. I have written this book to provide you with scriptural truths that will help you pray and think in ways that will transform your perspective to see God's good purpose in all that happens. Embracing these truths will enable you to remain right-side up instead of upside down! The immediate context of this book is set against the Corona Virus outbreak in 2020. But the biblical principles are timeless and have helped God's people throughout recorded time to remain faithful and upright in a turbulent world.

It is not the traumatic and sudden events of life that turn our world upside down, but rather our responses to these events that make all the difference and determine our perspective. Life becomes traumatic and overwhelming when we choose to follow our own natural responses instead of embracing God's perspective. Your daily prayer life plays a huge role in your ability to keep life-altering events from becoming life-dominating in a way that *really* turns your world upside down.

Allow me to offer a personal experience to illustrate this truth. In 2010, my wife, Ruth, was diagnosed with advanced Glioblastoma, the most lethal form of brain cancer. She embraced this diagnosis with gratitude to God and determined to live the rest of her life, however long that would be, to pray for and encourage others with God's faithfulness. Through excellent care from the Brain Cancer Center at Duke University, she lived another three and a half years. Not once during that time did I ever hear her say, "Why, me?" or anything close to it. She was fifty-six years old when she was diagnosed. She was a beautiful, faithful mother and wife. She was a brilliant Old Testament scholar. We had planned that she would be able to spend years teaching, writing, and encouraging people to train their children to love God's Word—but he had other plans. Ruth rejoiced in this new direction. Her life did not turn upside down. Rather, her faith has become a rock to many.

This is best illustrated by a precious memory that will always be engraved in my heart—the memory of the day Ruth told her mother about her diagnosis. Ruth's mom, Genevieve, is still alive today. Ruth was like her mom in that she was a woman of strong faith and minute-by-minute prayer. They both loved God's word. It was and is the foundation of their lives.

One afternoon in early April 2010, Ruth and I walked up to her mother's home to tell her what God was doing. I was confident that the conversation would go well. But I was totally blown away by what I heard. I listened in the kitchen as Ruth and her mom talked in the living room. They rejoiced at the good providence of God and were thrilled that they knew God had planned this moment before time began. They both took great comfort in the fact that God could be trusted. I heard joy, laughter, and praise that, at moments like these, their loving Sovereign God could be trusted. That moment was the result of both Ruth's and Genevieve's solid trust in the good providence of God. There were no tears that afternoon, except mine. These two women, living testimonies of faith, rested in the secure knowledge that their God was being faithful to them. They were comforted and secure in knowing they did not have to fear the days ahead.

This little book is all about how to walk before God in prayer and faith so that you will be able to remain right-side up when life appears to be upside down.

1

Who Controls Tomorrow

Do Humans Control Tomorrow?

Humans are obsessed with tomorrow. This obsession feeds the illusion that we can actually control tomorrow. In times when life is "normal," this illusion has an appearance of realism, much like a mirage in the desert. Thus, we act as though what we do actually controls what happens tomorrow. For example, if we spend all the money we have today, we won't have any money tomorrow. If we get good rest tonight, we will be better prepared for tomorrow. If we schedule wisely for the next day, it will likely be a more productive one. But these efforts to stay in control are only illusions that often dissolve in the busyness of life.

Jesus decisively put things in proper perspective against these illusions when he said,

Can any of you add one moment to his life span by worrying? If then you're not able to do even a little thing, why worry about the rest?

Luke 12:25–26

So much of the energy, money, and planning in our culture goes to extending our lives. But Christ tells us that we cannot even add an hour to our lives which, to him, is a very little thing. Rather, he challenges us to seek first the righteousness of the kingdom of God. Why? Because the events of tomorrow are in God's hands, not yours and not mine.

Think back with me to 9/11. In the space of a few hours, life all over the planet was radically changed by something that almost no one saw coming. Pearl Harbor in 1941, altered the course of world history in a single morning. Recently, the global spread of the Corona Virus has brought life to a virtual standstill with business forced to shut down, travel all but eliminated, and schools closed. The careful plans of people and institutions all over the planet for tomorrow have literally been turned upside down!

Despite all our careful planning and abilities as humans, we have to conclude that we do not control what happens tomorrow. This is our reality check. We are not in control!

This brings us back to the question that no one really wants to answer:

Who or What Is in Control of Tomorrow?

Many would answer there is no rational answer because all life is random. Nothing is predictable. Such thinking is debated in philosophy classrooms. But it is discounted by Christians and non-Christians alike who may say: "Everything happens for a reason." But of course, we want something more substantial than just a hopeful phrase when faced with something as ominous as a pandemic or large-scale "natural" disaster. You could go back to the philosophy classroom for answers or to the many deterministic theories, but you will not find any sense of peace or justice. Instead, you will only find more variations on the themes of random chance, hopeful karma, or blind fate. None of these new or ancient schemes will ease the agony of loss or mend a shattered dream. The hard truth is that randomness or determinism cannot offer comfort for troubled hearts.

So what is left? Just the enduring, beautiful truth that the healing hand of God controls tomorrow by his power and by his love. Over 2,700 years ago, the prophet Isaiah wrote these words about how God can be trusted:

Do you not know?
Have you not heard?
The LORD is the everlasting God,
the Creator of the whole earth.
He never becomes faint or weary;
there is no limit to his understanding.
He gives strength to the faint
and strengthens the powerless.
Youths may become faint and weary,
and young men stumble and fall,
but those who trust in the LORD
will renew their strength;
they will soar on wings like eagles;
they will run and not become weary,
they will walk and not faint.

Isaiah 40:28–31

The Living God knows about tomorrow and exactly what tomorrow will bring. His understanding is not limited by boundaries of human thought. In practice, this means that a virus or an earthquake is not a random event. We will go into this idea in more depth in the next chapter. Our focus in this opening chapter is to know the One who makes tomorrow happen. His acts are not random. He is not playing catch-up. Something like the Corona Virus Pandemic did not catch God by surprise. He was not on coffee break. If he is a God who keeps his word, then he knows all about tomorrow.

You see, Isaiah knew what the psalmist knew:

> All my days were written in your book and planned before a single one of them began.
> *Psalm 139:16b*

The Bible teaches about a loving, faithful, committed, honest God who controls tomorrow. This God cannot be bribed by wealth. He cannot be influenced by promises of fame.

The apostle Paul built on this reality when he was challenged about God's existence by the leading philosophers of Greece. Speaking before established and respected thinkers who knew little or nothing of his God, Paul chose to begin with God's power and his control over the events of all people. Rather than be timid or anxious about telling these intellectual giants about how powerful God is, Paul went right to the point of all human history. He told these great thinkers that his God not only determines where all people live, and not only does his God give everyone their next breath, but that he does all of this so that people would seek him and reach out for him. Paul tells them that this God they are asking him about is actually very near to them. Here is the exact answer that Paul gave some two thousand years ago:

> The God who made the world and everything in it—he is Lord of heaven and earth—does not live in shrines made by hands. Neither is he served by human hands, as though he needed anything, since he himself gives everyone life and breath and all things. From one man he has made every nationality to live over the whole earth and has determined their appointed times and the boundaries of where they live. He did this so that they might seek God, and perhaps they might reach out and find him, though he is not far from each one of us.
>
> *Acts 17:24–27*

What a beautiful expression of hope! Nothing is random. Whether you are facing a pandemic or are overwhelmed with dread for tomorrow, God has this. Tomorrow is not an unknown for him. Rather, tomorrow is filled with opportunities to reach out to the God who does all things well. You and I can trust his good care!

In the next chapter, we will examine how God controls the unexpected events of tomorrow to help us gain perspective for what is truly important in life.

2

When Life Turns Upside Down

The Power of the Earthquake

It was 5:36 p.m. March 27, 1964, Good Friday. At that moment, a 9.2 earthquake, the second largest ever recorded, struck the coast of Alaska near Anchorage. The shaking lasted for four minutes. The geological disruption was huge and devastating. The reason we don't know more about the history of the massive quake is that, at that time, very few people lived in that part of Alaska. The quake's impact was felt as far away as Louisiana, thousands of miles away! 131 people died as a result. If an earthquake of that magnitude had struck Seattle, San Francisco, or Los Angeles, the number of lives lost would have likely been in the tens of thousands, if not hundreds of thousands. This quake is a reminder that life can indeed turn upside down in the relative blink of an eye. It is naïve to think such an event could not happen again anywhere along the west coast of the United States.

Each geographic region on the planet faces similar catastrophic threats. The 2004 Christmas Indian Ocean tsunami, which killed over 250,000 people, is a case in point. Climate- and weather-related phenomena can bring immediate disruption of life and dreams. We are all vulnerable to sickness and the frailties of our bodies. And this, of course, is in addition to the capability of humans to spread disease and do violent harm to each other.

This leads us to consider three important realities:

THE FIRST REALITY: Upside-down moments are not rare; actually, they are to be expected! This means the upside-down moments are in fact a significant part of the fabric of everyday life.

THE SECOND REALITY: As we saw in the previous chapter, God is in control of the upside-down events of your life. Stated another way, God's idea of *normal* is much different than our idea of *normal.*

THE THIRD REALITY: God is in the middle of life's upside-down moments. This means that you can know peace and be secure when they come. Building on the first two realities, the reason for our being stressed when life turns upside down is directly connected to our being falsely convinced that God must do what *we* think is best.

With these three realities in place, let's examine God's control of the weather to help us form a framework that will guide our hearts to respond with wisdom and peace when our lives get turned upside down.

What could give us a more clear and awesome display of God's power than the weather? Meteorological events can bring about sudden and radical change. One moment a house is standing and the next it is not. This life-altering event is not caused by chance or bad luck; it is caused by the powerful hand of God at work.

The Holy Spirit's wisdom shown in Job 37:1–16 is a great place to start as it highlights the mighty hand of God at work in the sky, and shows us what a proper response looks like. Here is the passage with some comments that will enable us to construct this framework.

Living in Awe and Respectful Fear of God's Greatness and Power (vv. 1–5)

Has a sudden crash of thunder ever made your heart leap, or the brilliance of a bolt of lightning erupting in the night sky ever taken your breath away? God's great power is always on display in the weather! The power of a storm and the gentleness of a summer breeze display both the ferocity and the gentleness of God's character. The intense combinations of wind, thunder, and lightning demonstrate just how vulnerable we are before the Lord of heaven and earth.

> My heart pounds at this
> and leaps from my chest.
> Just listen to his thunderous voice
> and the rumbling that comes from his mouth.
> He lets it loose beneath the entire sky;
> his lightning to the ends of the earth.
> Then there comes a roaring sound;
> God thunders with his majestic voice.
> He does not restrain the lightning
> when his rumbling voice is heard.
> God thunders wondrously with his voice;
> he does great things that we cannot comprehend.
>
> *Job 37:1–5*

Understanding Why, Even if Only a Little
(vv. 6–13)

Verses 7 and 13 provide us at least a glimpse as to why God moves as he does with the weather. *He wants us to stop what we are doing and acknowledge his greatness and majesty.* When there is a heavy snowfall, our first response should not be to acquire a vehicle that will not be stopped by the snow. That may be a good idea, but our first response should be to recognize that God is at work with the heavy snowfall or downpour of rain. These events are not just obstacles to overcome. God wants all people to see that they are accountable to him. Verse 13 states that rain, whether gentle or flooding, is not random. God's purposes are being carried out as he intended.

In verses 11 and 12, the Holy Spirit reminds us that even the movements of the clouds are not random. They are moving at his careful direction. I find great comfort and delight in watching the clouds, knowing that God is intentionally choreographing each movement.

> For he says to the snow, "Fall to the earth,"
> and the torrential rains, his mighty torrential
> rains, *serve as his sign to all mankind,*
> *so that all men may know his work.*
> (Emphasis added.)

The wild animals enter their lairs
and stay in their dens.
The windstorm comes from its chamber,
and the cold from the driving north winds.
Ice is formed by the breath of God,
and watery expanses are frozen.
He saturates clouds with moisture;
he scatters his lightning through them.
They swirl about,
turning round and round at his direction,
accomplishing everything he commands them
over the surface of the inhabited world.
He causes this to happen for punishment,
for his land, or for his faithful love.
(Emphasis added.)

Job 37:6–13

Making Wonder and Humility Habits
of the Heart (vv. 14–16)

These last three verses bring the proper perspective.
We will never have all the answers, but we are always
in awe before God's wonders. We don't have the
answers to the big questions that we long for and are
even desperate for. It is a futile quest to demand to
know what only God knows. But here, in these few
words, the Holy Spirit tells us what we need to know.

God does control the immense power of the weather. And in humility, these wonders should cause us to pause and stand in meekness before the Great God of Heaven.

> Listen to this, Job.
> Stop and consider God's wonders.
> Do you know how God directs his clouds
> or makes their lightning flash?
> Do you understand how the clouds float,
> those wonderful works of him who has perfect knowledge?
>
> *Job 37:14–16*

With these biblical truths in place, we can be ready to face the traumatic events and sudden changes in our lives. The foundation for this framework is that *we must live in continual awe of our dependence upon God's great power.* This is not a one-time realization that occurs but rather a continual, daily habit of the heart. The very next breath you take is an indication of God's sustaining care for your life. Wow! That is a game changer for most of us. If you had a narrow escape with something that was life-threatening or something that took your breath away, you would be quick to acknowledge God's protection. But taking the next breath should be just as dramatic for us.

Next, even though we don't know all of the reasons why traumatic events happen, we do know that *God is in control of them,* just as he is in control of the weather. Therefore, we know just enough of the "why" to be content with God's care.

The last part of the framework is humility. It is not our place to question or challenge God when our lives turn upside down. Instead, we can choose to honor him by applying the framework of responses the Holy Spirit gave us in Job 37.

- Living in continual awe and respectful fear of God's greatness and power;
- Trusting that God is in control and being content with his care;
- Making wonder and humility habits of heart.

Of course, as humans, this framework is not our natural response. Our natural response is one of fear. This is the subject of the next chapter.

3

The Fear Factor

Fear and Emotional Protection

When Adam chose to disbelieve God and instead believe in himself, he exposed the entire human race to a deadly emotional contagion called fear. Humans are not designed to fear anything or anyone but God. We are made in God's image to experience complete trust and security in our relationship with him. Fear robs us of that trust. Fear eats away at us. Fear destroys trust and leads us into the deceptive world of self-reliance and emotional chaos. As is obvious, fear thrives when life turns upside down!

How do you combat the fear of upside-down moments?

The answer is that fear comes from misplaced trust. When we trust ourselves, we invite fear to dominate the upside-down events of life. In sharp contrast, Psalm 33:20–22 says:

> We wait for the LORD;
> he is our help and shield.
> For our hearts rejoice in him
> because we trust in his holy name.
> May your faithful love rest on us, LORD,
> for we put our hope in you.
>
> *Psalm 33:20–22*

When your trust is placed in God, you put fear in the proper perspective. In this life, we will never be able to totally eradicate fear. However, as the psalmist urges, we can turn to God who is always trustworthy. This psalm commands God's people not to trust things of human origin for safety or as a refuge from fear. A king should not trust the size of his army or the warrior his great strength. The mighty war horse is a false hope for deliverance.

Wait, What?

Are not these the very things that are supposed to produce victory in battle? Actually, no! Verses 18–19 offer these words as the real hope for safety:

> But look, the LORD keeps his eye on those who
> fear him—
> those who depend on his faithful love
> to rescue them from death
> and to keep them alive in famine.
>
> *Psalm 33:18–19*

Fear comes when we don't see God as our hope and our place of safety. This is the practical application from the previous chapter. When we direct our fear away from people and things, and move towards the fear of the Living God of the Bible, we are secure, no matter the outcome of the battle.

In Psalm 33, the one who trusts in God—who places his hope in God—forms a barrier of emotional protection around his heart. Our emotions flow from our thoughts. Job feared the Lord and shunned evil. By loving God, loving his word, and loving his care for us, we begin to build an emotional bond of trust. Pursuing God in this way with all of our hearts is the only way to cause our emotions to work for us rather than against us. This is why Jesus says that greatest commandment is to love God with everything that we have to give. See Matthew 22:37–40.

The pursuit of truth with your whole heart will reorient your thinking so that you do not give in to the fear that life's traumatic events bring. Love of God's truth will transform your thoughts and produce emotions that will not cave in under the pressure of the chaotic, unexpected moments of life.

One passage in particular that will work to diminish the fear factor you inherited from Adam is Romans 8:28–39. Here are three foundational truths that will build your trust in God:

The FIRST truth is found in Romans 8:28:

> *We know that all things work together for the good of those who love God, who are called according to his purpose.* (Emphasis added.)

When facing unexpected, life-disrupting moments, this truth is your anchor. No matter what happens, God's eternal purpose is to use that event for good. If you are driven by fear, these words will have little comfort for you and these events will send you into a tailspin. However, if you daily train your thoughts to embrace the fact that God *does* work all things together for his glory and your good, you will quickly see God's hand in even the most stressful events of life.

The SECOND truth is found in Romans 8:31:

> *What then are we to say about these things? If God is for us, who is against us?* (Emphasis added.)

These words bring the truth of Psalm 33 home to our hearts. The eyes of the Lord are indeed on his people. And if God is for us, nothing can escape his eyes that stand watch over us. This makes his care personal, close, and intentional, even when life turns tragically traumatic! This has the capacity to bring great comfort to a heart whose thoughts have been trained to think God's thoughts after him. With this type of compassionate, competent, loving care, fear is lessened. It no longer dominates. You are one step closer to being freed from the dominance of fear. However, there is one final truth that seals your heart and prepares it for the world you inhabit.

This THIRD truth is found in Romans 8:37–39:

> *No, in all these things we are more than conquerors through him who loved us. For I am persuaded that neither death nor life, nor angels nor rulers, nor things present nor things to come, nor powers, nor height nor depth, nor*

any other created thing will be able to separate us from the love of God that is in Christ Jesus our Lord. (Emphasis added.)

You see, you are more than someone who has seen and knows the truth. You are more than someone who is wonderfully cared for by God. You are also more than even a conqueror when it comes to defeating the challenge of fear. These words assure you of God's care *and* of God's victory! There is nothing that can separate you from the love of God.

By rebuilding your thoughts to be consistent with these truths from Psalm 33 and Romans 8, you will rebuild your emotional responses to be aligned with God's truth instead of your fears. This will bring the stability you need to not to be controlled by fear when life turns upside down.

Now that the fear factor has been put in perspective, we have to stop the blame game.

4

The Dangerous Blame Game

The Game That Comes Naturally

When something tragic or unfortunate happens, our first response is often to find someone or something to blame. Judgments are quickly made, tempers flare, relationships are damaged or lost because there "must" be someone to blame for such a painful outcome. This is one reason why the Holy Spirit forbids us to make rash or quick judgements. While there are some devastating events that can be linked to a specific cause or person, the vast majority cannot. Thus, much time and energy may be spent in nonproductive pursuits and anger that drain us both physically and spiritually. The blame game is self-destructive!

When we assign blame to a circumstance that turns life upside down, we are throwing all of the truths we have encountered earlier in this book out the window. The culture around us has chosen not to believe that the human race is cursed by the fall. So there is a refusal to account for the impact of sin upon our lives. This is especially true when large-scale tragic events happen. Thus, when one of these events occurs, there is typically a pattern of trying to assign blame after the fact. *This leads to speculation and blaming that obscures the real issue—our rebellion against God.*

Jesus brings a clear understanding to the futility of this blaming mentality. Luke records an exchange that addresses the danger of assigning blame in these situations.

At that time, some people came and reported to him about the Galileans whose blood Pilate had mixed with their sacrifices And he responded to them, "Do you think that these Galileans were more sinful than all the other Galileans because they suffered these things? No, I tell you; but unless you repent, you will all perish as well. Or those eighteen that the tower in Siloam fell on and killed—do you think they were more sinful than all the other people who live in Jerusalem? No, I tell you; but unless you repent, you will all perish as well."

Luke 13:1–5

The first verse is referring to some Galileans who were killed by Pilate for improper activity at the temple. Apparently, some were attempting to say they deserved to die. This is why Jesus says in verse 2: "Do you think that these Galileans were more sinful than all the other Galileans because they suffered these things?" This is the question we are all tempted to ask when we attribute suffering to specific causes and we ignore the impact of the fall and sin.

Jesus then resoundingly answers his own question this way: "No, I tell you; but unless you repent, you will all perish as well." Just because there is suffering does not mean we can establish immediate blame and ignore the curse of sin. Jesus then references eighteen people who died when a tower fell on them. Are they more guilty than everyone else in Jerusalem? What Christ is saying, in effect, is that if those eighteen died because they were guilty, everyone in Jerusalem is guilty and should also die.

Christ is teaching us that when we see suffering as in these two events, rather than assigning blame, *we should be seeking God with broken, repentant hearts.*

Your ability to quickly see the need for repentance will keep your life from being dominated by feelings of dread and despair—that life makes no sense. Living with a humble and repentant heart will bring you deep peace and life-giving joy. It will keep you from viewing your world through lenses that are upside down.

Our natural inclination since the fall is to blame. Adam got things horrifically wrong, of course, when he blamed his wife and God for his sin. We are still following his example. The blame game is not safe at all.

This leads us to the next chapter: just how big a deal is the fall?

5

Understanding the Fall

The Groaning Creation

The fall of the human race is almost exclusively ignored by modern culture. The idea that the entire human race is born guilty of sin and exists in rebellion against a holy God before whom we are all deemed accountable is both laughable and repugnant. So, the belief that the fall impacts the entire planet and reaches into every area of life is seen as even more far-fetched. The cultural influence of this thinking warps both our thinking and our practices. Modern geology, history, anthropology, sociology, and psychology, etc., have no place for the fall. So, we tend to ignore that the fall is an important component of our everyday lives, particularly when events and circumstances overwhelm us. However, ignoring the fall will cause you to have a falsely positive perception of the condition of the world around you. This is even true for the physical world. The fall has left its ugly mark everywhere under the sun.

The apostle Paul is not shy about referring to the fall and its impact on creation. He tells us that all of creation is longing, groaning to be set free from the deadly, decaying legacy of the fall. Here are Paul's words:

> For the creation eagerly waits with anticipation for God's sons to be revealed. For the creation was subjected to futility—not willingly, but because of him who subjected it—in the hope that the creation itself will also be set free from the bondage to decay into the glorious freedom of God's children. For we know that the whole creation has been groaning together with labor pains until now.
>
> *Romans 8:19–22*

These words from Paul build upon the truth found in Psalm 98. The psalmist also connects the physical creation to the sin of man and the fall. Through the Holy Spirit, he says the physical creation is longing to rejoice at the coming of the Messiah who will make all things right. This gives the song *Joy to the World* a rich and significant theme.

> Let the sea and all that fills it,
> the world and those who live in it, resound.
> Let the rivers clap their hands;
> let the mountains shout together for joy
> before the LORD,
> for he is coming to judge the earth.
> He will judge the world righteously
> and the peoples fairly.
>
> *Psalm 98:7–9*

Understanding the pervasiveness of the influence of the fall underscores one of the principles set forth in chapter 2 of this book:

> *"Upside-down moments are not rare; actually they are to be expected! This means that the upside-down moments are actually a significant part of the fabric of everyday life."*

The reality of the fall means that our planet and its people will continue to groan under the weight of sin until Christ returns. Thus, it is an unrealistic assertion to proceed on the belief that our lives will be trouble free. Indeed, we would be safer to proceed on the belief that we exist in a hostile environment and engage in daily combat. We are citizens of another country—a heavenly country. We must not expect this place where we live now to supply everything that we need and desire. Relief from the weight of sin and the fall will not happen on this planet.

But take heart, there is real encouragement here! Yes, the fall is real. But the good news is that *even in the hard sufferings of life, we can know the peace and healing of God right here and now.* Christ directs us in the Lord's Prayer to call for God's kingdom to expand on earth as it is already established in heaven. Your faith in God here on earth strikes against the legacy of the fall and extends all the way to heaven itself.

Along these lines, Paul encourages us with these words:

Therefore we do not give up. Even though our outer person is being destroyed, our inner person is being renewed day by day. For our momentary light affliction is producing for us an absolutely incomparable eternal weight of glory. So we do not focus on what is seen, but on what is unseen. For what is seen is temporary, but what is unseen is eternal.

2 Corinthians 4:16–18

We will examine this truth in much more detail in chapter 7.

But as we close this chapter, you must reassess whether you have been influenced to discount the reality of the fall in your life and in the world around you. This impact was so profound, so massive, that only the death of the holy Son of God could end its terrible reign.

In the next chapter, we will see how history has been shaped by upside-down events.

6

Perspective

Throughout History, God Remains Faithful
to His Promise

God's purpose in history is to gather a people together who would follow him so that all the peoples of the earth would be blessed. This was the covenant promise God gave to Abram in Genesis 12:3. It has sustained the people of God for the last 4,000 years. Indeed, God tells Abram that all the people of the earth will be blessed and protected through Abram.

That the promise which describes how all of human history will unfold for the next 4,000 years is "tucked away" in a single line of Hebrew poetry is mind-blowing to us. As people who are both flawed and finite, we would expect that something this important should be told to us on every page of the Bible and reinforced by visions and daily prophetic pronouncements! But God, who is infinite and without flaw, only has to state his intention once, and it will happen whether we get it or not.

God protects and blesses all of mankind through the descendants of Abraham. That is reality. Once again, there is no support for this belief in modern culture. This kind of thinking is deemed strange, medieval, or, at best, archaic. But regardless of popular consensus, this is reality. This is truth. All of the milestone moments in history that have blessed and protected mankind were put in place either by the people of God or orchestrated by God to protect his people so that humans as a race would be protected and blessed. That is mind-blowing!

Okay, so now we have some context for what the title of this chapter means. We have context for understanding that what appear to be upside-down events are actually opportunities for God's people to see that life is really right-side up.

Through the prophet Isaiah, God pulls back the curtain and allows us to get a behind-the-scenes view of God putting his purpose and plans into action. In Isaiah 45:1–7, God describes how he is using Cyrus, king of Persia, to bring about his plan.

In verses 1–3, we see how he is using Cyrus to accomplish his purposes. As verse 4 states, Cyrus is not a willing participant. And notice also in verse 4 that God clearly states that he is doing these things for his people, just as he said he would in Genesis 12:3.

The LORD says this to Cyrus, his anointed,
whose right hand I have grasped
to subdue nations before him
and disarm kings,
to open doors before him,
and even city gates will not be shut:
"I will go before you
and level the uneven places;
I will shatter the bronze doors
and cut the iron bars in two.
I will give you the treasures of darkness
and riches from secret places,
so that you may know that I am the LORD.
I am the God of Israel, who calls you by your name.
I call you by your name,
for the sake of my servant Jacob
and Israel my chosen one.
I give a name to you,
though you do not know me.
I am the LORD, and there is no other;

there is no God but me.
I will strengthen you,
though you do not know me,
so that all may know from the rising of the sun
to its setting
that there is no one but me."

Now, one more point from this portion of Isaiah. Notice what God says in verse 7. God is the one who creates both prosperity and disaster.

I form light and create darkness,
I make success and create disaster;
I am the LORD, who does all these things.

Isaiah 45:1–7

This is how God operates in history. This is how God has always acted to remain faithful to his promise. This provides some context for what God is doing in massive global events like the 2020 Corona Virus Pandemic. Just as he did with Cyrus, God is bringing about all of the many strands of the pandemic so that all mankind may know that God is the Lord, the King, and that we are all accountable to him. Just as Cyrus was unaware that he was God's anointed to accomplish God's purpose, so the major players in this pandemic are also unaware.

There are so many events happening on the global stage dominated by many good and bad actors alike that everything appears to be upside down. But for God and his people, everything is right-side up. This is how understanding the purposes of God, as he permits us to know them in his Word, provides us with the confidence that we are secure in God's good providence. As we live through the unsettling quarantine, the financial uncertainties, and the legitimate health concerns, we can be confident of God's good care and his love. It is true: everything is right-side up!

Here are some final thoughts from the book of Daniel to set the historical perspective:

Daniel praised the God of the heavens and declared:
May the name of God
be praised forever and ever,
for wisdom and power belong to him.
He changes the times and seasons;
he removes kings and establishes kings.
He gives wisdom to the wise
and knowledge to those
who have understanding.
He reveals the deep and hidden things;

he knows what is in the darkness,
and light dwells with him.

Daniel 2:19b–22

God is the one who has control over the affairs of people, pandemics, and powers. Put your trust in God. Rest in peace during the dramatic upside-down moments. Know that even in these uncertain times, God is faithfully keeping his promise to bring blessing to the families of the earth.

In the next chapter, we will explore how life really is right-side up.

7

When Upside Down is Really Right-Side Up

So There Is Good News!

This chapter is, for me, the most satisfying one of this book. It has the message that thrills my heart. It has been a challenge for me to wait this long to share it with you! However, if I had begun with this chapter, its powerful message might have seemed superficial and overly optimistic. But now the foundation has been laid that is able support the full weight of these glorious truths. Let's begin by looking at Psalm 23.

Psalm 23 is frequently read at funerals and graveside services. While this is appropriate, this beautiful psalm of David is even better suited for everyday life. If you will recall the memory of my wife, Ruth, and her mom, from the introduction to this book, they found their joy in the comfort that God was always caring for them. They knew that Christ was their Shepherd. They knew he was right there with them, caring for them, loving them, and that they had no reason to fear. Even if there were dangers and dark clouds swirling around them, they knew they were secure in the hands of their Shepherd Savior.

This is where Psalm 23 begins. The Lord of heaven and earth is my Shepherd. He is keeping his good promise made to Abraham. We do have all that we need! Ah, I can almost hear someone saying, *I need to pay my bills, I have plenty of needs. How do I have all that I need?* That is a fair question! David is not attempting to address the matter of physical provision. He is saying that the Lord is his Shepherd. He knew that his God would be with him. He had everything that he needed to honor God as he walked through the darkest valleys of life. That day when Ruth and her mom were rejoicing, they were resting in the lush green pastures of their Shepherd King. They were nourished by the quiet, gentle stream flowing through the pasture. They were joyful because their hearts were blessed that Christ, their Shepherd, was leading them along a path that would bring honor to him. They had everything they needed.

If you remove this reality from that conversation, you would be left with heartbreak and despair—a mother knowing that she would soon lose her daughter; a daughter with such amazing gifts to give would be left wondering if it was all worth it. They would have faced the desperation of an upside-down life with no hope.

But, praise God, this Psalm was their reality. They truly were in the Shepherd's good care.

> The LORD is my shepherd;
> I have what I need.
> He lets me lie down in green pastures;
> he leads me beside quiet waters.
> He renews my life;
> he leads me along the right paths
> for his name's sake.
>
> *Psalm 23:1–3*

This psalm never loses touch with the reality of the fallen world. It speaks to the harsh realities of life. It is language in which David acknowledges that he must pass through the dark, dark valleys of a sin-cursed world. However, he never forgets that he is in the constant care of his Shepherd. He is confident that the rod and the staff of his God will defeat the enemies he will face. Like David, Ruth and Genevieve found comfort as they faced danger in life's darkest valley.

Even when I go through the darkest valley,
I fear no danger,
for you are with me;
your rod and your staff—they comfort me.

Psalm 23:4

David rejoiced in the goodness of God. He knew that because of the faithfulness of his God to keep his covenant promises, he was richly blessed. Despite the fact that everything around him indicated his life was upside down, he knew, by faith, that he was blessed beyond measure. He knew his life was secure in God's faithfulness. He knew that he was not pursued by fear, but by the faithful, relentless love of the good Shepherd.

You prepare a table before me
in the presence of my enemies;
you anoint my head with oil;
my cup overflows.
Only goodness and faithful love will pursue me

all the days of my life,
and I will dwell in the house of the LORD
as long as I live.

Psalm 23:5–6

Psalm 23 is about everyday life. Its message brings stability, comfort, and peace. Whether you face a pandemic, a tragic loss of someone close, or the devastation of an earthquake, you are cared for by the Shepherd who calls you to lie down in his good, green pastures.

This comforting truth is expressed many times in the Psalms, perhaps most beautifully in Psalm 73. In the final three verses, we find what it means to view life in the stability of God's faithfulness. These words embrace everything we have looked at so far.

Even when our bodies fail—even when our hearts are overwhelmed with the harshness of life—God continues to be our strength. Even when it appears that evil is winning and things appear upside down, God will not lose. That means that we will not lose! This is true because the nearness of God is our good. He will remain faithful to us so that we can bring hope to ourselves and to those close to us.

My flesh and my heart may fail,
but God is the strength of my heart,
my portion forever.
Those far from you will certainly perish;
you destroy all who are unfaithful to you.
But as for me, God's presence is my good.
I have made the Lord GOD my refuge,
so I can tell about all you do.

Psalm 73:26–28

Finally, let's return to 2 Corinthians. These words are the perfect summary for this chapter. Ruth and Genevieve did not lose hope because their eyes were fixed on what is unseen. What we can see with our eyes—what we can experience with our senses—is not all that there is. Actually, it is only a small portion of what life is about. Paul acknowledges that things may appear to be upside down. However, only when our eyes are fixed upon what is unseen can we grasp what is really going on. Paul urges us to look to the eternal reality. This is what brought joy to my wife and her mom!

Therefore we do not give up. Even though our outer person is being destroyed, our inner person is being renewed day by day. For our momentary light affliction is producing for us an absolutely incomparable eternal weight of glory. So we do not focus on what is seen, but on what is unseen. For what is seen is temporary, but what is unseen is eternal.

2 Corinthians 4:16–18

Now you can see why this chapter is so precious to me. The nearness of God is our good. He is our loving Shepherd. We are secure in him as we live for the glory of God.

This leads us straight to the gospel!

8

The Gospel is Your Anchor

The Lord Renews Your Strength

How is the gospel an anchor in a pandemic or an earthquake? Christians die just as easily as anyone else. Exactly! Upside-down events point to the common ground that we all share as humans: we all die. We are all vulnerable to sickness, injury, and loss. The gospel adds the missing, unseen dimension to the trauma of life-altering events. As we saw in the last chapter, the unseen realities are more secure and more certain than what we can see and perceive with our senses. We need the lens of the gospel to access this unseen dimension. This is what provides the ability to hope when challenges are looming. We will still know grief, but, as Paul also reminds us, our grief is not like those who do not have the hope of the gospel. Once again, the Psalms provide the perspective to make the gospel the anchor that will keep us secure and right-side up. A huge component in remaining stable and knowing peace is gratitude.

Psalm 103 shows the importance and power of gratitude. If you are not overflowing with gratitude to God for his goodness to you in Christ, he will only be like Santa Claus to you—someone you get things from, not someone you serve, honor, or praise.

The psalm begins with a bold invitation to praise God with every fiber of your being. It is this wholehearted devotion to daily gratitude and praise that prepares your heart for the challenging, unexpected moments that lie ahead. This is where the gospel is immense in its impact. David begins by combining praise with gratitude. David is inviting us to be fully engaged in praise by remembering all the benefits God has lavished upon us. This needs to be a constant theme of our hearts in order to establish healthy emotional habits of grace that keep our focus on the sufficiency of God's grace.

My soul, bless the LORD,
and all that is within me, bless his holy name.
My soul, bless the Lord,
and do not forget all his benefits.

Psalm 103:1–2

The first thing David offers for praise is God's forgiveness for all of our sins. This is why the gospel forms the basis of gratitude and results in stability and peace in life. The gospel redeems every part of our lives. God reaches down into the pit of our dark struggles. He doesn't just say it is going to be okay. No, he crowns us with love and compassion in ways that are truly beyond anything we can imagine. We are satisfied from the bounty of the Lord's table that we saw in Psalm 23. The rich, nutritional harvest from his table renews us with the strength of eagles. This gospel-based understanding prepares us to have the vision and faith we need to see life right-side up.

> He forgives all your iniquity;
> he heals all your diseases.
> He redeems your life from the Pit;
> he crowns you with faithful love and compassion.
> He satisfies you with good things;
> your youth is renewed like the eagle. . .
>
> *Psalm 103:3–5*

Another precious benefit of the gospel is that we experience daily the compassion and grace of God instead of his anger! This is huge. The Holy Spirit reminds us in the Proverbs and in the letter to the Hebrews that the Lord disciplines those whom he loves. He does not accuse or treat our lack of love for him as we deserve to be treated. Instead, he separates us from the guilty consequences of sin. Because of the gospel, the consequences we receive for our sins are in the form of loving discipline and not the harsh weight of his wrath. So while the Lord's discipline may be painful at times, it always draws us back to him in love. This is so important to grasp. When the difficulties come that appear to turn life upside down, remember that because of the far-reaching impact of the gospel, you can *know and be assured* that you are receiving loving discipline and not judgmental wrath. (See Hebrews 12:5–11.)

> The LORD is compassionate and gracious,
> slow to anger and abounding in faithful love.
> He will not always accuse us
> or be angry forever.
> He has not dealt with us as our sins deserve
> or repaid us according to our iniquities.
> For as high as the heavens are above the earth,
> so great is his faithful love
> toward those who fear him.
> As far as the east is from the west,
> so far has he removed
> our transgressions from us.
>
> *Psalm 103:8–12*

The gospel affords us another special grace in challenging times—the comforting rest of Christ.
In Matthew's Gospel, Christ also makes an invitation much like David did in Psalm 103. He invites you to come to him when you are exhausted by the trials that come when things appear to be upside down. His invitation is, of course, for any who are weary and tired, but it is especially appropriate for the huge emotional and physical drain that comes from dealing with a viral pandemic or devastating "natural" disaster.

Jesus' invitation comes with a condition. It is a gracious condition, but a condition nonetheless: the way to rest and have peace is to take Christ's yoke upon the shoulders of your heart and be led by him. A yoke is a device that was placed on the necks of oxen to keep them moving in the right direction, whether it was to grind grain or plow a field. The yoke was necessary to keep them in line. The yoke of Christ, instead of being harsh and uncomfortable, is soft and easy to wear. But, make no mistake about this, it is still designed to keep us moving in the right direction; to keep us from going our own way. Without this yoke, we would go our own way, straight to disaster. This is the yoke given by the Holy Spirit in his Word designed to deliver us from evil and temptation.

If you will accept this loving, gracious, essential

condition and follow the ways of your Savior, you will know true peace and rest. Your burden will be the light burden of the gospel and not the harsh consequences of sin and punishment. Christ's words are your hope and peace when the enemy wants to turn your world upside down. These are the life-giving words of Christ that form the anchor you need to remain right-side up!

> Come to me, all of you who are weary and burdened, and I will give you rest. Take up my yoke and learn from me, because I am lowly and humble in heart, and you will find rest for your souls. For my yoke is easy and my burden is light.
>
> *Matthew 11:28–30*

This brings us to next and final chapter; your future is secure!

9

Your Future Is Secure

Death Is Swallowed Up in Victory

We have come to the last chapter. There is one topic remaining that needs to be addressed directly and clearly. That is the topic of death. The way that we respond to death is a major reason why life can become upside down. As the last chapter acknowledged, no one is immune to death. It happens to all of us. By building on the solid foundation of the gospel, let's examine what the Holy Spirit wants you to know and think about death.

In American culture, awareness of death, in the last 160 years, has become less prominent because of better health care, lower infant mortality rates, and living and working conditions that are safer and more sanitary than in the past. According to www.statista.com, the average life expectancy in the United States in 1860 was 39.4 years. Today it is just under 79 years, almost double the expectancy in 1860. In America and other places, we are living longer, and this may feed the delusion that we can evade death. The fear of life being turned upside down by massive-scale events or "freak" accidents is common to most and an obsession for many others.

God's answer to this fear is the message of the gospel. The gospel opens the door to the eternal, unseen world that allows you and me *not* to be dominated by fear. Because death is a legitimate universal to all people, the truths in this short book can form a point of contact with nearly everyone you encounter to be able to talk about the practical reality of the gospel.

Paul takes the issue of death head-on in all his writings, but he does so explicitly in the fifteenth chapter of 1 Corinthians. Here is a summary of some of his thoughts regarding death:

In verse 19 he concludes a discussion about the resurrection of Christ by saying: "If only for this life we have hope in Christ, we are to be pitied more than all men." If we live as the culture does, without hope of the resurrection, Paul says we are a sorry lot. Ignoring the reality of Christ conquering death means that we ignore the heart of what it means to be a Christian. *If we fear death the way the world around us fears death, we will be a miserable mess and our testimony to others about the upside-down events of life will have little impact.* We will be disconnected from what we say we believe.

A few more sentences later in the chapter, Paul returns to the relevance of the resurrection. In verses 32 and 33 he says: "If the dead are not raised, "Let us eat and drink, for tomorrow we die." Do not be misled: "Bad company corrupts good character." If we don't view death the way the Holy Spirit does, why even bother with issues like holiness and obedience? Party tonight for tomorrow could be all there is. Paul warns that this kind of disregard for Christ's conquering death and this kind of ignorance of the unseen, eternal world will corrupt our thinking. This is why you must not let influences that are not invested in the power of the gospel affect the way you view a pandemic or the other life-altering events we have been discussing.

Then lastly, and most significantly, read how Paul ends the magnificent chapter. Here are verses 54–58:

> When this corruptible body is clothed with incorruptibility, and this mortal body is clothed

with immortality, then the saying that is written will take place:

Death has been swallowed up in victory.

Where, death, is your victory?

Where, death, is your sting?

The sting of death is sin, and the power of sin is the law. But thanks be to God, who gives us the victory through our Lord Jesus Christ!

Therefore, my dear brothers and sisters, be steadfast, immovable, always excelling in the Lord's work, because you know that your labor in the Lord is not in vain.

1 Corinthians 15: 54–58

This triumphant claim by Paul is that the power of death has ended. This is the amazing reality that will keep your life and your world right-side up. The sting of death, whether through a pandemic, tsunami, tornado, sickness, or tragic accident, is softened, and through Christ, is victorious no more. When there are large numbers of deaths, it appears as if death and evil have won. But Paul reclaims the victories of death and, because of the gospel, cancels out the victory of the grave.

In Christ, your future is secure. The unseen reality of eternity is real and constant. Nothing that claims to turn your world upside down will stand. Paul's finishing words bring comfort and lasting peace. No event or circumstance can rob you of the security you have in Christ. This is the message God calls you to believe when life attempts to turn everything upside down.

Allow me to end where we began. This book is about living life from God's perspective, and not your own. This cannot not happen without consistent, informed, faithful prayer. Praying constantly for God's wisdom and discernment is a lifestyle habit that will keep your world balanced. Your heart can remain right-side up, regardless of the circumstances you encounter.

> Now to him who is able to do above and beyond all that we ask or think according to the power that works in us—to him be glory in the church and in Christ Jesus to all generations, forever and ever. Amen.
>
> *Ephesians 3:20–21*

Appendix 1

Teach Your Children to Live Right-Side Up

Your children live in a culture that is truly upside down. God is irrelevant or mocked in the news media. Prayer is illegal in schools. He has been removed from the history books. The idea of sin and accountability to a holy, righteous God is absent from our government. Pandemics and catastrophic events are connected to random chance, geological and meteorological phenomena, and human error. Your children live in a world that offers no comfort when tragic, unexpected loss occurs.

The biblical truths of this small book offer the hope, comfort, and understanding to know peace and rest when life seems to be upside down. Do not wait until a catastrophic event happens to talk to your children about God's interaction with their world. Here are some ways you can prepare your children to remain right-side up in a turbulent world.

Live out the principles of the book in your own life. As the saying goes, you cannot give what you don't have. Children know when we are being genuine. The truth of Deuteronomy 6 directly applies here. Whatever is on your heart will be transmitted to their hearts. Ask God for a heart of humility so that, when challenging events come, your faith in his care and goodness will be impressed deeply on the hearts of your children.

Speak openly and frequently about how God is always caring for your family. Your everyday talk is the most important tool you have to prepare your children for the uneven, upending events of life. Reinterpret what the news media say about why things happen. The Bible is full of stories, illustrations, and commands that speak to the events of everyday life, both good and tragic. Thank God for a safe trip to the store or for a good day at school. This will help prepare both you and your children for the challenges that will come.

Use the Bible references in the book to begin building your set of passages that speak to upside-down situations. The truths given in the book are not exhaustive. Engage your pastor and trustworthy resources to build a "toolbox" of truth that fits where you live and where your family finds itself in life. The same principles apply, no matter where you are, but the application of these truths may be quite different, depending on where you live. Someone living on the west coast of the United States will have differing applications to those who live in Switzerland or Singapore. The single mom will need to deploy these truths differently than the parents of a two-parent home.

Invest the time necessary to deeply know your children. Your children's lives are marked by rapid change. It is vital that you know them well enough to see when an upside-down event has happened in their life. Events that take place that you are not aware of are shaping them in significant ways. Invest in your children and delight in them so that you can help them be right-side up instead of upside down. Think back to your own childhood and remember how many times you felt alone or confused but were afraid to talk with your parents. Make things different for your children. Follow God's example and become a place of safety and refuge for your children when they need it most.

Dominate your life with the constant, joyous praise of God. The psalmist teaches us to make your life about praise. As one popular song says, learn to praise him in the storm! Your children know the difference between genuine and superficial praise. Fill your heart and the lives of your children with abundant praise of the great God of heaven.

These ideas are just the beginning. Lead your children to a place of comfort and safety. Jesus teaches that the catastrophic storms of life happen to the wise and the foolish alike. Build your house upon the foundation of these truths so that when the storms come, you and your house will remain standing right-side up.

Appendix 2

Comfort for Your Community

The New York Times has proclaimed that America has become a *Xanex* nation. It is true: our culture is dominated by anxiety, worry, and fear. The fears are only deepened in the face of pandemics and tragedies; the times when life turns upside down.

You will recall that in chapter three we saw that *"Fear comes when we don't see God as our hope and our place of safety."* Embracing God as your rock and refuge means that you will stand out in sharp relief from those around you in your community. News reports, presidential proclamations, updates from respected scientists and doctors will not bring peace and comfort. We have seen this dramatically illustrated in the Corona Virus pandemic. It appears that the more information that is given, the more anxiety increases. People don't need more information! They need truth!

Trusting God's truth means you find comfort in his Word, not in more information or changing circumstances. You have the opportunity to let your trust in God's good providence transform you to be salt and light in an uncertain world. Don't hide your trust in God under a basket! This trust is a light that is to demonstrate the power of the gospel to those in your community, your church, and your own home. Your faith in God's control and his purposes will bring hope to those gripped by fear.

As we learned from Job 37, these unexpected, unsettling events are from God so that we will stop our everyday labors and acknowledge his greatness. As those who have been redeemed from the fears of this world, we have the opportunity and the obligation to tell people that none of these events is random.

Of course, this is only possible if you actually do believe God's truth and live it out. If you are anxious, irritable, easily angered, and on edge, your words will have little impact. You will only be salt and light when you stand calm and confident—as you remain right-side up in the face of a pandemic. Of course, you will be concerned about the impact of a deadly virus, but your concerns will be radically different than the concerns of a world that has no fear of God or love of his providence.

God has made you to be a light! You can show your weakness and concern. You can acknowledge that sickness or death is not something you want for yourself or others. But you can do this in a way that shows that your dependence on God is a genuine expression of faith and trust in him. This is how you can connect to those who struggle with anxiety. You can be a source of light in the face of fear and darkness by showing those around you that God is the source of your strength and peace. You can be a light in a dark, trembling world.

We wait for the LORD;
he is our help and shield.
For our hearts rejoice in him
because we trust in his holy name.
May your faithful love rest on us, LORD,
for we put our hope in you.

Psalm 33:20–22

About Shepherd Press Publications

They are gospel driven;
They are heart focused;
They are life changing.

Our Invitation to You

We passionately believe that what we are publishing can be of benefit to you, your family, your friends, and your work colleagues. So we are inviting you to join our online mailing list so that we may reach out to you with news about our latest and forthcoming publications, and with special offers.

Visit:

www.shepherdpress.com/newsletter

and provide your name and email address.

Also by Jay Younts

Everyday Talk
Talking Freely and Naturally about God with Your Children

978-0-97230-469-6

Paperback | 160pp

"*This book is amazingly practical and refreshingly biblical. It reminds us that our everyday talk influences our children greatly.*"
Lance and Beth Quinn

Also by Jay Younts

Everyday Talk about Sex and Marriage
A Biblical Handbook for Parents

978-1-63342-087-8

Paperback | 80pp

*"There is not a parent wouldn't benefit greatly from
this book. This is a wise, winsome, gospel-soaked
and practical manual of how to talk to your kids
about sex as you live with them in a world that's gone
sexually insane. Don't wait, order this book now."*
Paul David Tripp

About Jay Younts

John A. (Jay) Younts is the author of this book as well as other materials on parenting and the Christian life. He is an experienced blogger, having served Shepherd Press in this capacity for several years. He has been teaching and speaking on current issues for over thirty years. He serves as a ruling elder at Redeemer Associate Reformed Presbyterian Church in Moore, South Carolina. He and his late wife, Ruth, have five adult children.

Follow Jay on Social Media

YouTube Channel: EverydayTalk 24/7
www.everydaytalk247.com
Facebook: https://www.facebook.com/jay.younts
Twitter: @wordsmatter247
jayyounts@gmail.com

To buy copies of this book in bulk at a special discounted price, inquire from the publishers.